Data Science Toolbox
for Beginners

Learn Essential tools like Pandas, Dask,
Numpy, Matplotlib, Seaborn, Scikit-learn,
Scipy, TensorFlow/Keras, Plotly, and More

i

Data Science ToolBox for Beginners

Learn Essential tools like Pandas, Dask, Numpy, Matplotlib, Seaborn, Scikit-learn, Scipy, TensorFlow/Keras, Plotly, and More

Emmanuel Anuoluwa Bamidele Ph.D.

Data Science ToolBox

First published: 2024

ISBN: 9798874171407

PREFACE

This book is written for those who are new to the field, eager to learn about data science, and ready to get hands-on with the essential tools and techniques.

If you're starting from scratch, looking to familiarize yourself with relevant data science libraries, and aspiring to undertake data science and machine learning projects independently, you have the right book. This book will introduce you to Python, a language loved for its ease of learning and powerful capabilities in data analysis. We'll explore foundational libraries such as NumPy, Pandas, Dask, and essential visualization tools like Matplotlib, Seaborn, and Plotly.

But we won't stop there. You'll also learn introductory level machine learning using Scikit-learn and some deep learning with TensorFlow and Keras. To complement your data science skills, we'll also provide a refresher or introduction to statistical analysis, an indispensable part of understanding and working with data.

Finally, we'll round up your learning journey by highlighting and walking you through the data science project lifecycle. This book isn't just about learning concepts; it's about applying them. You'll finish with the confidence and knowledge to start your projects, from framing the problem to writing your solutions.

So, whether you're a complete beginner or looking to brush up on your skills, let this book be your guide. Even after you have finished using it, trust me, you will always have to come back to it at any level in your data science career. Let's embark on this journey together, transforming curiosity into expertise, one page at a time.

INTRODUCTION

This book is designed as a reference for Python's most powerful and popular libraries used in data science, offering an in-depth exploration of their functionalities and applications.

Data science, an interdisciplinary field, is at the forefront of extracting knowledge and insights from data. It encompasses various techniques from statistics, machine learning, data analysis, and computer science, all aimed at analyzing and interpreting complex digital data. The role of Python in this domain has been pivotal due to its simplicity and the robust ecosystem of data-oriented libraries.

This guide is not just about Python as a programming language; it's a compass to navigate the extensive toolkit that Python offers for data science. Each chapter of this book is dedicated to a specific library, delving into its core functionalities, methods, and how they can be applied to real-world data science problems.

Whether you are a beginner looking to understand the basics of libraries like NumPy, Pandas, Matplotlib, Seaborn, Plotly, Dask, or an experienced practitioner interested in advanced topics like machine learning with Scikit-learn and deep learning with TensorFlow or Keras, this book offers a detailed look into the tools that make Python a leader in data science.

The knowledge you will acquire by using this book include:

1. Basic introduction to python with examples, enough to get you going for data science libraries in this book.
2. The foundational libraries for numerical computing and data manipulation.

3. Libraries that bring statistical methods and machine learning to your fingertips.

4. Visualization tools to make sense of your data graphically.

5. Advanced libraries for specialized tasks in scientific computing and more.

By the end of this guide, you will have a solid understanding of how to leverage Python's extensive library ecosystem to analyze, visualize, and interpret data effectively. Let's embark on this journey to master the tools that empower data science in Python.

CHAPTER 1 : BASIC PYTHON FOR DATA ANALYSIS

Setting up Python and Jupyter Notebook

Here's a step-by-step guide:

Step 1: Download Anaconda

1. **Visit the Anaconda Website:** Go to Anaconda's official website.

2. **Choose the Correct Version:** Select the installer for your operating system (Windows, macOS, or Linux). Choose the Python 3.x version, as it's the most up-to-date.

Step 2: Install Anaconda

1. **Run the Installer:** After downloading, run the installer.

2. **Follow the Installation Prompts:** Accept the license agreement. Choose an install location (the default should be fine for most users). Optional: You may be prompted to install Microsoft VSCode. Choose based on your preference.

3. **Complete the Installation:** Once the installation is complete, you can finish and exit the installer.

Step 3: Verify Installation

1. **Open Anaconda Navigator:** Search for Anaconda Navigator in your applications and open it.

2. **Check for Python and Jupyter:** The Navigator GUI should show Python and Jupyter Notebook as available applications.

Step 4: Launch Jupyter Notebook

1. **From Anaconda Navigator:** Click on the Jupyter Notebook icon to launch it. This will open Jupyter Notebook in your default web browser.

2. **From Command Line or Terminal:** Alternatively, you can open a command prompt or terminal and type **jupyter notebook**. This also opens Jupyter Notebook in your web browser.

Step 5: Create a New Notebook

1. **In the Jupyter Interface:** Click on "New" at the top right corner. Select "Python 3" to create a new notebook.

Step 6: Using Jupyter Notebook

1. **Write and Execute Code:** Type Python code into a cell. Press **Shift + Enter** or **Command + Enter** to execute the code in the cell.

2. **Save and Exit:** Save your notebook with the save icon. Close the browser tab to stop the notebook.

3. **Shut Down the Jupyter Kernel:** If you launched from the Anaconda Navigator, shut it down from there. If you used the command line, return to the command prompt or terminal and press **Ctrl + C**, then confirm to shut down the server.

Note: for all installations of libraries in this book, we use pip which is used in terminals. However, if you want to use it in **Jupyter Notebook**, you need to add "!". i.e :

!pip instead of pip

Python Syntax and Concepts

We start with the iconic "Hello, World!" program to understand how Python executes code. We then explore essential elements like variables, basic data types (integers, floats, strings, and booleans), and operators for arithmetic and comparison. These foundational concepts are important as they form the building blocks of more complex Python programming.

Write your first python code:

```
print("Hello, World!")
Hello, World!
```

Variables and Basic Types

In Python, variables are used to store data values. They act like containers for data, allowing you to label and store different types of information that your program can manipulate. There's no need to declare a variable's type explicitly; Python automatically determines the type based on the assigned value.

Python supports various basic data types:

1. **Integers (int):** These are whole numbers without a fractional component, like **5**, **100**, or **-3**. They can be of any length and aren't limited by size, only by available memory.

2. **Floating Point Numbers (float):** These are numbers that include a decimal point, such as **3.14**, **2.0**, or **-0.001**. Floats in Python are akin to double in languages like C or Java.

3. **Strings (str):** Strings are sequences of characters, used to store text. They are enclosed in quotes, for instance, **"Hello"**, **"Data Science**

101". Python strings are immutable, meaning once created, their contents can't be changed.

4. **Booleans (bool):** This type represents the truth values of logic. They can be either **True** or **False**. Booleans are often the result of comparison operations and are extensively used in control structures like if-else statements.

```python
x = 5           # integer
y = 3.14        # float
name = "Emmanuel" # string
is_valid = True  # boolean
```

```python
print(x, y, name, is_valid)
```

```
5 3.14 Emmanuel True
```

Basic Operators

```python
# Arithmetic Operators
x = 10
y = 3
print("Arithmetic Operators:")
print("Addition (x + y):", x + y)   # 13
print("Subtraction (x - y):", x - y)   # 7
print("Multiplication (x * y):", x * y)   # 30
print("Division (x / y):", x / y)   # 3.333...
print("Modulus (x % y):", x % y)   # 1
print("Exponentiation (x ** y):", x ** y)   # 1000
print("Floor Division (x // y):", x // y)   # 3

# Comparison Operators
print("\nComparison Operators:")
print("x > y is", x > y)   # True
print("x < y is", x < y)   # False
print("x == y is", x == y)   # False

# Assignment Operators
print("\nAssignment Operators:")
x += 2   # Equivalent to x = x + 2
print("x after x += 2:", x)   # 12

# Logical Operators
print("\nLogical Operators:")
print("x > 5 and y < 5 is", x > 5 and y < 5)   # True
print("x < 5 or y < 5 is", x < 5 or y < 5)   # True
print("not(x < 5) is", not(x < 5))   # True

# Identity Operators
print("\nIdentity Operators:")
a = y
print("a is y:", a is y)   # True
print("a is not x:", a is not x)   # True

# Membership Operators
print("\nMembership Operators:")
list = [1, 2, 3, 4, 5]
print("y in list:", y in list)   # True
print("x not in list:", x not in list)   # True
```

The answer we obtain will be:

```
Arithmetic Operators:
Addition (x + y): 13
Subtraction (x - y): 7
Multiplication (x * y): 30
Division (x / y): 3.3333333333333335
Modulus (x % y): 1
Exponentiation (x ** y): 1000
Floor Division (x // y): 3

Comparison Operators:
x > y is True
x < y is False
x == y is False

Assignment Operators:
x after x += 2: 12

Logical Operators:
x > 5 and y < 5 is True
x < 5 or y < 5 is True
not(x < 5) is True

Identity Operators:
a is y: True
a is not x: True

Membership Operators:
y in list: True
x not in list: True
```

Data Structure

Data structures are fundamental in programming, allowing you to organize and store data efficiently. This section introduces Python's primary data structures: lists, dictionaries, tuples, and sets. You'll learn how to create and manipulate these structures, such as adding or accessing elements. Understanding these data structures is vital for handling and analyzing data in Python.

Lists

Lists in Python are versatile and widely used data structures that store sequences of items. Lists are Defined by square brackets **[ ]** with items separated by commas. They are mutable, meaning you can modify them after creation, and can hold a variety of data types, including a mix of integers, strings, floats, and even other lists. Here's a concise overview of lists in Python:

```python
# Creating a list
my_list = [1, 2, 3, 'Python', 3.14]
print("Original List:", my_list)

# Accessing list elements
print("First Element:", my_list[0])   # Accessing the first element
print("Last Element:", my_list[-1])   # Accessing the last element

# Modifying the list
my_list.append('New Item')   # Appending a new item
print("After Append:", my_list)
my_list[1] = 'Changed'   # Changing the second element
print("After Modification:", my_list)

# Slicing a list
sliced_list = my_list[1:4]   # Slicing from second to fourth element
print("Sliced List:", sliced_list)

# List Comprehension
doubled_list = [x * 2 for x in [1, 2, 3]]   # Doubling each element in a new list
print("Doubled List:", doubled_list)

# Nested Lists
nested_list = [1, 2, ['Nested', 'List'], 4]
print("Nested List:", nested_list)

# Common Operations
print("Length of List:", len(my_list))   # Length of the list
concatenated_list = my_list + ['Extra', 'Elements']   # Concatenating lists
print("Concatenated List:", concatenated_list)

# Iterating over a list
print("Iterating over the list:")
for item in my_list:
    print(item)
```

```
Original List: [1, 2, 3, 'Python', 3.14]
First Element: 1
Last Element: 3.14
After Append: [1, 2, 3, 'Python', 3.14, 'New Item']
After Modification: [1, 'Changed', 3, 'Python', 3.14, 'New Item']
Sliced List: ['Changed', 3, 'Python']
Doubled List: [2, 4, 6]
Nested List: [1, 2, ['Nested', 'List'], 4]
Length of List: 6
Concatenated List: [1, 'Changed', 3, 'Python', 3.14, 'New Item', 'Extra', 'Elements']
Iterating over the list:
1
Changed
3
Python
3.14
New Item
```

Dictionary

Dictionaries in Python are unordered collections of data values that are used to store data values like a map. Dictionaries are defined with curly braces { } containing key:value pairs. Their keys must be unique and immutable. Values can be of any data type. Unlike other Data Types that hold only a single value as an element, Dictionary holds key:value pairs. Here's a concise overview:

```python
# Creating a dictionary
my_dict = {'name': 'Alice', 'age': 25}
print("Original Dictionary:", my_dict)

# Accessing elements
print("Name:", my_dict['name'])
print("Age:", my_dict.get('age'))

# Modifying the dictionary
my_dict['age'] = 26  # Updating value
my_dict['address'] = '123 Street'  # Adding new key-value pair
print("Modified Dictionary:", my_dict)

# Removing elements
my_dict.pop('address')
print("After Removing Address:", my_dict)

# Iterating through a dictionary
print("Iterating through the dictionary:")
for key, value in my_dict.items():
    print(key, ":", value)

# Dictionary Comprehension
squared_dict = {x: x**2 for x in range(6)}
print("Dictionary Comprehension (squared values):", squared_dict)

# Nested Dictionary
nested_dict = {'dict1': {'key1': 'value1'}, 'dict2': {'key2': 'value2'}}
print("Nested Dictionary:", nested_dict)

# Common Operations
print("Length of Dictionary:", len(my_dict))
print("Keys of Dictionary:", my_dict.keys())
print("Values of Dictionary:", my_dict.values())
```

```
Original Dictionary: {'name': 'Alice', 'age': 25}
Name: Alice
Age: 25
Modified Dictionary: {'name': 'Alice', 'age': 26, 'address': '123 Street'}
After Removing Address: {'name': 'Alice', 'age': 26}
Iterating through the dictionary:
name : Alice
age : 26
Dictionary Comprehension (squared values): {0: 0, 1: 1, 2: 4, 3: 9, 4: 16, 5: 25}
Nested Dictionary: {'dict1': {'key1': 'value1'}, 'dict2': {'key2': 'value2'}}
Length of Dictionary: 2
Keys of Dictionary: dict_keys(['name', 'age'])
Values of Dictionary: dict_values(['Alice', 26])
```

Tuples

Tuples in Python are similar to lists, but they are immutable, meaning once defined, their elements cannot be changed. They are Defined with parentheses ( ) with items separated by commas. Tuples are an important data type, especially when you need a sequence of items that should not be modified. Here's an overview:

```python
# Creating tuples
my_tuple = (1, 'Hello', 3.14)
another_tuple = 2, 'Python'
print("Original Tuple:", my_tuple)
print("Another Tuple:", another_tuple)

# Accessing tuple elements
print("Second Element of my_tuple:", my_tuple[1])

# Tuples are immutable, so you cannot change, add, or remove elements after creation
# my_tuple[1] = 'World' would result in an error

# Slicing tuples
sliced_tuple = my_tuple[0:2]
print("Sliced Tuple:", sliced_tuple)

# Nested tuples
nested_tuple = (1, (2, 3), ['a', 'b'])
print("Nested Tuple:", nested_tuple)

# Tuple unpacking
a, b, c = my_tuple
print("Unpacked:", a, b, c)

# Common Operations
print("Length of my_tuple:", len(my_tuple))
concatenated_tuple = my_tuple + another_tuple
print("Concatenated Tuple:", concatenated_tuple)
print("Is 3.14 in my_tuple:", 3.14 in my_tuple)
```

```
Original Tuple: (1, 'Hello', 3.14)
Another Tuple: (2, 'Python')
Second Element of my_tuple: Hello
Sliced Tuple: (1, 'Hello')
Nested Tuple: (1, (2, 3), ['a', 'b'])
Unpacked: 1 Hello 3.14
Length of my_tuple: 3
Concatenated Tuple: (1, 'Hello', 3.14, 2, 'Python')
Is 3.14 in my_tuple: True
```

Sets

Sets in Python are collections that are unordered and unindexed. **Sets are** defined with curly braces **{}** with elements separated by commas. Alternatively, can be created using the **set()** function. They are used to store unique elements, meaning they automatically eliminate any duplicates. Here's a concise overview of sets:

```python
# Creating sets
my_set = {1, 2, 3, 'Python'}
another_set = set(['a', 'b', 'c'])
print("Original Set:", my_set)
print("Another Set:", another_set)

# Sets are unique, duplicates are removed automatically
duplicate_set = {1, 2, 2, 3}
print("Set with Duplicates Removed:", duplicate_set)

# Accessing set elements: Cannot access by index, but can iterate
print("Iterating through the set:")
for item in my_set:
    print(item)

# Checking membership
print("Is 'Python' in my_set:", 'Python' in my_set)

# Adding elements
my_set.add('new')
print("After adding an element:", my_set)
my_set.update([4, 5])
print("After updating with multiple elements:", my_set)

# Removing elements
my_set.discard(4)
print("After discarding an element:", my_set)

# Set Operations
set1 = {1, 2, 3}
set2 = {3, 4, 5}
print("Union of set1 and set2:", set1 | set2)
print("Intersection of set1 and set2:", set1 & set2)
print("Difference of set1 and set2:", set1 - set2)
print("Symmetric difference of set1 and set2:", set1 ^ set2)

# Immutable Sets
immutable_set = frozenset([1, 2, 3])
print("Immutable Set:", immutable_set)
```

```
Original Set: {1, 2, 3, 'Python'}
Another Set: {'a', 'c', 'b'}
Set with Duplicates Removed: {1, 2, 3}
Iterating through the set:
1
2
3
Python
Is 'Python' in my_set: True
After adding an element: {1, 2, 3, 'Python', 'new'}
After updating with multiple elements: {1, 2, 3, 4, 5, 'Python', 'new'}
After discarding an element: {1, 2, 3, 5, 'Python', 'new'}
Union of set1 and set2: {1, 2, 3, 4, 5}
Intersection of set1 and set2: {3}
Difference of set1 and set2: {1, 2}
Symmetric difference of set1 and set2: {1, 2, 4, 5}
Immutable Set: frozenset({1, 2, 3})
```

File Handling

File handling is a critical skill in python for reading data from files and writing output to files. This section covers how to open, read, write, and close files in Python. We focus on text files and demonstrate these operations using the **open** function with different modes like "read" (r) and "write" (w). Practical examples show how to handle files gracefully, ensuring data is correctly processed and stored.

Writing and Reading a File

In Python, reading from and writing to files is a straightforward and essential task, especially in data processing and analysis. Python's built-in functions make it easy to handle various file operations with minimal code. Here's a brief introduction:

Writing to a File:

- This involves creating a file or opening an existing file in write (**'w'**) mode and then writing data to it.

- The **write()** method is used to insert content into the file.

- Opening a file in write mode automatically creates the file if it doesn't exist or overwrites it if it does.

Reading from a File:

- This involves opening a file in read (**'r'**) mode to access its content.

- Methods like **read()**, **readline()**, and **readlines()** are used to retrieve file content.

- **read()** returns the entire content, while **readline()** and **readlines()** are useful for reading lines individually or as a list, respectively.

Using the with Statement:

- The **with** statement in Python is used for resource management and ensures that the file is properly closed after its operations are completed.

- It automatically handles exceptions and resource deallocations, making code cleaner and more readable.

File Paths:

- When dealing with files, specify the correct file path. Paths can be absolute or relative to the current working directory.

```python
# Python code snippet demonstrating reading from and writing to a file

# Writing to a file
with open('write_example.txt', 'w') as write_file:
    write_file.write("Hello, Python!\n")
    write_file.write("Writing to files is simple.")

# Reading from the same file
with open('write_example.txt', 'r') as read_file:
    content = read_file.read()
    print("File Content:\n", content)
```

Error Handling

Error handling is essential for writing robust and reliable Python programs. The examples in this section teaches you how to gracefully catch and respond to exceptions in Python using try-except blocks. You'll learn about common exceptions like **ZeroDivisionError** and **FileNotFoundError**. We also discuss the **finally** block, which is executed regardless of whether an error occurred, typically used for clean-up actions like closing files.

```python
try:
    result = 10 / 0
except ZeroDivisionError:
    print("Divided by zero!")
```

```python
try:
    file = open("example.txt")
    content = file.read()
except FileNotFoundError:
    print("File not found.")
finally:
    file.close()
```

CHAPTER 2 : NUMPY

Introduction to NumPy

NumPy, standing for Numerical Python, is a foundational library in Python's data science ecosystem. It's lauded for its high-performance multi-dimensional array object and an extensive collection of mathematical functions. NumPy forms the backbone of many other Python scientific libraries, enabling efficient numerical computations.

Installation

```
pip install numpy
```

Array Creation and Manipulation

NumPy's primary object is the homogeneous multi-dimensional array. Arrays can be created directly from Python lists or using built-in functions:

```
import numpy as np
a = np.array([1, 2, 3])  # One-dimensional array
b = np.array([[1.5, 2.5], [3.5, 4.5]])  # Two-dimensional array
```

Reshaping arrays:

```
c = np.array([[1, 2], [3, 4], [5, 6]])
c = c.reshape(2, 3)  # Reshapes c to a 2x3 array
```

Mathematical Operations

NumPy supports a wide range of mathematical operations. Element-wise operations are straightforward:

```
x = np.array([1, 2, 3])
y = np.array([4, 5, 6])

# Elementwise sum, difference, product
print(x + y)   # [5 7 9]
print(x - y)   # [-3 -3 -3]
print(x * y)   # [4 10 18]

[5 7 9]
[-3 -3 -3]
[ 4 10 18]
```

NumPy also excels in handling more complex mathematical operations like matrix multiplication:

```
a = np.array([[1, 2], [3, 4]])
b = np.array([[5, 6], [7, 8]])
print(np.dot(a, b))   # Matrix multiplication

[[19 22]
 [43 50]]
```

Linear Algebra Functions

NumPy's linear algebra capabilities are extensive, enabling operations from simple vector arithmetic to complex matrix transformations:

```
x = np.array([[1, 2], [3, 4]])

# Compute the inverse
print(np.linalg.inv(x))

[[-2.   1. ]
 [ 1.5 -0.5]]
```

Solving linear equation systems

```
# Solve the system ax = b
a = np.array([[3, 1], [1, 2]])
b = np.array([9, 8])
x = np.linalg.solve(a, b)
print(x)

[2. 3.]
```

Statistical Methods

NumPy's statistical tools offer insights into data. Basic descriptive statistics are readily available:

```
data = np.array([1, 2, 3, 4, 5])

# Calculate mean, median, and standard deviation
mean = np.mean(data)
median = np.median(data)
std_dev = np.std(data)
print(mean, median, std_dev)
```

```
3.0 3.0 1.4142135623730951
```

For more advanced statistical analysis, functions like correlation coefficients are essential:

```
x = np.array([1, 2, 3])
y = np.array([4, 5, 6])
print(np.corrcoef(x, y))
```

```
[[1. 1.]
 [1. 1.]]
```

Handling Multi-Dimensional Data

A significant strength of NumPy is its ability to effortlessly handle multi-dimensional data, making it indispensable for image processing, 3D visualizations, and complex simulations:

```
# Creating a 3D array
z = np.random.rand(2, 3, 4)  # 2x3x4 array with random numbers
print(z)
```

```
[[[0.52587419 0.30288669 0.50037786 0.97692273]
  [0.65977242 0.49967761 0.00914506 0.6034636 ]
  [0.65362012 0.68967435 0.41667024 0.75796993]]

 [[0.63341878 0.1038912  0.31786011 0.64657894]
  [0.78933222 0.18664426 0.06957168 0.55678476]
  [0.32714702 0.28639153 0.21337103 0.96699523]]]
```

Integration with Other Libraries

NumPy seamlessly integrates with other libraries in the Python data ecosystem, like Pandas for data manipulation, Matplotlib for plotting, and Scikit-learn for machine learning. This interoperability makes NumPy a versatile tool in a data scientist's toolkit.

CHAPTER 3: PANDAS - DATA MANIPULATION AND ANALYSIS

Introduction to Pandas

Pandas, a library built on top of NumPy, is a powerhouse in data manipulation and analysis for Python. It provides high-level data structures and functions designed to make data analysis fast and easy. With its core structures, Series and DataFrames, Pandas is well-suited for different kinds of data such as tabular, ordered and unordered time series, arbitrary matrix data, among others.

Installation

pip install pandas

Data Structures: Series and DataFrames

At the core of Pandas are the Series and DataFrame objects. A Series is a one-dimensional array-like object containing a sequence of values and an associated array of data labels, called its index.

```
import pandas as pd
s = pd.Series([1, 3, 5, np.nan, 6, 8])  # Creating a Series
print(s)
0    1.0
1    3.0
2    5.0
3    NaN
4    6.0
5    8.0
dtype: float64
```

A DataFrame is a two-dimensional, size-mutable, and potentially heterogeneous tabular data structure with labeled axes (rows and columns).

```python
data = {'Name': ['John', 'Anna', 'Peter', 'Linda'],
        'Age': [28, 34, 29, 32]}
df = pd.DataFrame(data)  # Creating a DataFrame
df.head() #to view to five rows
```

	Name	Age
0	John	28
1	Anna	34
2	Peter	29
3	Linda	32

Data Importing and Exporting

Pandas can read and write data in a wide variety of formats including CSV, Excel, SQL databases, and HDF5.

```python
# Reading a CSV file
file_directory = r"/xxxx/Codes/BNB Historical Data - Investing.com2015_to_2022.csv"
df = pd.read_csv(file_directory)
df.head()
```

	Date	Price	Open	High	Low	Vol.	Change %
0	16-Feb-22	430.80	432.31	433.28	427.90	1.09M	-0.33%
1	15-Feb-22	432.21	403.49	441.20	402.70	1.24M	7.12%
2	14-Feb-22	403.49	397.83	404.20	390.61	500.69K	1.43%
3	13-Feb-22	397.80	403.22	407.02	394.90	426.23K	-1.34%
4	12-Feb-22	403.20	400.16	406.90	393.59	569.68K	0.78%

You can export the DataFrame after cleaning or working on it.

```python
# Writing to an Excel file
df.to_excel('filename.xlsx', sheet_name='Sheet1')
df.to_csv('filename.xlsx', index=True)
df.to_
    to_clipboard
    to_csv
    to_dict
    to_excel
    to_feather
    to_gbq
    to_hdf
    to_html
    to_json
    to_latex
```

Data Cleaning and Transformation

Data cleaning and transformation are vital in data analysis. Pandas offers numerous built-in functions for data cleaning, like handling missing data, dropping columns, and replacing values.

```python
# Filling missing data
df.fillna(value=5)

# Dropping columns
df.drop('column_name', axis=1, inplace=True)
```

Pandas provides robust methods for dealing with missing data. **isna()** and **dropna()** can be used to identify and remove null values, respectively.

```python
# Identifying missing data
df.isna()

# Dropping rows with missing data
df.dropna(how='any')
```

Pandas also allows for robust transformations, that is you can apply a function to a column.

```python
# Applying a function to data
df['new column name'] = df['column'].apply(lambda x: x + 1)
```

Grouping and Aggregation

Grouping data based on certain criteria and then applying an aggregate function is a common operation. Pandas provides the **groupby** method for this purpose.

```python
# Grouping and then applying the sum function to the grouped data
df.groupby('category_column').sum()
```

For complex data sets, advanced grouping with multiple keys and applying different aggregation functions is possible.

```
# Grouping by multiple columns
df.groupby(['col1', 'col2']).mean()

# Applying multiple aggregation functions
df.groupby('col').agg({'data1': 'mean', 'data2': 'sum'})
```

Pivot

Pivoting a DataFrame in Pandas is a way to reshape or transform the data. It can turn unique values from one column in the original data into multiple columns in the output, with data reshuffled accordingly. This is particularly useful for creating a more readable and organized format of the data.

```
import pandas as pd

# Sample data in a DataFrame
data = {'Date': ['2021-01-01', '2021-01-01', '2021-01-02', '2021-01-02'],
        'User': ['Emmy', 'Bams', 'Ayo', 'Deji'],
        'Score': [23, 45, 32, 67]}

df = pd.DataFrame(data)
df
```

	Date	User	Score
0	2021-01-01	Emmy	23
1	2021-01-01	Bams	45
2	2021-01-02	Ayo	32
3	2021-01-02	Deji	67

```
# Pivoting the DataFrame
pivot_df = df.pivot(index='Date', columns='User', values='Score')

pivot_df
```

User	Ayo	Bams	Deji	Emmy
Date				
2021-01-01	NaN	45.0	NaN	23.0
2021-01-02	32.0	NaN	67.0	NaN

The **pivot_df** is the transformed DataFrame (**df**) created by employing the **pivot** method. In this pivoted structure, the unique entries from the 'Date' column of the original DataFrame are transformed into the row indices. Simultaneously, the distinct values from the 'User' column are rearranged to

31

form the column headers. The cells of this newly shaped DataFrame are then populated with the corresponding values from the 'Score' column, aligning each user's score with the appropriate date.

<u>Melt</u>

Pandas' **melt** function is used for transforming or reshaping data. It turns columns into rows, effectively 'melting' the DataFrame. This is particularly useful when you need to change a DataFrame from a wide format to a long format.

```python
import pandas as pd
# Sample data in a DataFrame
data = {'Date': ['2021-01-01', '2021-01-02'],
        'Emmy': [23, 32],
        'Bams': [45, 67]}

df = pd.DataFrame(data)
df
```

	Date	Emmy	Bams
0	2021-01-01	23	45
1	2021-01-02	32	67

```python
# Melting the DataFrame
melted_df = df.melt(id_vars=['Date'], var_name='User', value_name='Score')
melted_df
```

	Date	User	Score
0	2021-01-01	Emmy	23
1	2021-01-02	Emmy	32
2	2021-01-01	Bams	45
3	2021-01-02	Bams	67

The **melted_df** is a DataFrame created by utilizing the **melt** function, which restructures the original data from the df DataFrame. Within this transformation, **id_vars=['Date']** serves to maintain the 'Date' column as an identifier variable, keeping it unchanged. The parameter **var_name='User'** establishes a new column named 'User', where the original column headers

'Emmy' and 'Bams' are transformed into row entries. Simultaneously, **value_name='Score'** designates the name for a new column where the values from the initial 'Emmy' and 'Bams' columns are reorganized and aligned, effectively transforming the DataFrame from a wide format to a long format with these adjustments.

Pandas' **pivot_table** is also a powerful tool that provides Excel-like functionalities to create summary tables.

```
# Creating a pivot table
table = pd.pivot_table(df, values='D', index=['A', 'B'],
                        columns=['C'], aggfunc=np.sum)
```

The function **pd.pivot_table** is used to create a new table that organizes the data from the original DataFrame **df** into a grid that provides a multidimensional summary of the data.

In the operation shown, **pd.pivot_table** takes the **df** DataFrame and aggregates the values under column 'D'. These values are grouped based on unique combinations found in columns 'A' and 'B', which are set as the new row indices. Simultaneously, the unique values in column 'C' are used to create the new columns of the pivot table.

The aggregation function applied here is the sum (**np.sum**), meaning that for each group created by the unique combinations of 'A' and 'B', and for each unique value in 'C', the function will calculate the total sum of the corresponding values in 'D'.

Joining and Merging

Combining multiple datasets is a common operation. Pandas offers various methods for merging and joining DataFrames.

```
# SQL-style joins
result = pd.merge(df1, df2, on='key')

# Concatenating along an axis
result = pd.concat([df1, df2], axis=1)
```

Visualization

Pandas integrates with Matplotlib for basic plotting functionality, allowing for quick visualizations of the data.

```
# Plotting directly from DataFrame
df.plot(kind='bar')
```

Performance Tuning

For large datasets, Pandas offers options like chunking large files, using efficient data types, and parallel processing to improve performance.

```
# Reading a file in chunks
chunk = pd.read_csv('file.csv', chunksize=1000)
```

Scalability with Dask

For very large datasets, Pandas can be used in conjunction with Dask, a parallel computing library, to scale computation.

```
import dask.dataframe as dd
dask_df = dd.from_pandas(df, npartitions=10)
```

CHAPTER 4: DASK FOR SCALABLE DATA ANALYSIS

Introduction to Dask

Dask is an open-source library for parallel computing in Python that seamlessly integrates with existing NumPy, Pandas, and Scikit-Learn workflows. It is designed to operate in parallel on single machines or across a cluster, scaling from laptops to clusters seamlessly. Dask enables performance at scale, handling larger-than-memory datasets through its efficient use of computation and streaming algorithms.

Why Use Dask?

When dealing with large datasets, traditional Python libraries like Pandas can become slow or even fail to process the data due to memory constraints. This is where Dask, an open-source parallel computing library, becomes necessary. Dask is specifically designed to work with large datasets that exceed the memory capacity of a single machine. It achieves this by breaking down large computations into smaller, manageable chunks, which are then executed in parallel across multiple cores or even different machines. This approach not only allows for handling larger datasets efficiently but also speeds up the processing time significantly.

Dask is compatible with many of the familiar data structures in Pandas and NumPy, making it a natural choice for users who need to scale their data processing tasks. It provides parallelized versions of common Pandas and NumPy functions, enabling users to apply the same syntax and operations they are accustomed to, but on larger datasets and with greater computational efficiency.

Installation

pip install dask

pip install dask-ml

pip install s3fs #to use with s3 bucket

Core Components of Dask

Dask consists of two components: dynamic task scheduling and big data collections. The task scheduler executes task graphs with low overhead, while the big data collections include Dask DataFrame, Dask Array, Dask Bag, and Dask Delayed which mimic their Pandas, NumPy, and Python counterparts.

Dask Arrays

Dask arrays coordinate many NumPy arrays, arranged into chunks within a grid. They support a large subset of the NumPy API, which makes it easy to use in existing projects.

```
import dask.array as da
x = da.random.random((10000, 10000), chunks=(1000, 1000))
y = x + x.T
z = y[::2, 5000:].mean(axis=1)
z.compute()
```
```
array([1.00034712, 0.99174431, 0.99786351, ..., 0.9973064 , 0.9987624 ,
       0.9949985 ])
```

Dask DataFrames

Dask DataFrames are large parallel DataFrames composed of many smaller Pandas DataFrames, split along the index. They support a large chunk of the Pandas API.

```
import dask.dataframe as dd
file_directory = r"xxx/Books/Data Science Toolbox/Codes/BNB Historical Data - Investing.com2015_to_2022.csv"
df = dd.read_csv(file_directory)
df.head()
```

	Date	Price	Open	High	Low	Vol.	Change %
0	16-Feb-22	430.80	432.31	433.28	427.90	1.09M	-0.33%
1	15-Feb-22	432.21	403.49	441.20	402.70	1.24M	7.12%
2	14-Feb-22	403.49	397.83	404.20	390.61	500.69K	1.43%
3	13-Feb-22	397.80	403.22	407.02	394.90	426.23K	-1.34%
4	12-Feb-22	403.20	400.16	406.90	393.59	569.68K	0.75%

Using Dask Delayed

Dask's **delayed** function is a simple and powerful way to parallelize existing Python code. It makes functions lazy, meaning they don't execute their computations immediately. Instead, they record what they were called with and build up a task graph. This task graph captures the sequence of operations, allowing Dask to later run these operations in parallel efficiently.

This approach is particularly effective for parallelizing existing codebases or complex computations that don't fit into the standard array/dataframe model.

How it works:

Decorate Functions: By using the **@delayed** decorator or wrapping a function call with **delayed()**, you tell Dask to delay the execution of the function. Instead of executing immediately, the function will wait to compute its result until explicitly told to do so.

Build a Task Graph: When delayed functions are called, they return lazy **Delayed** objects. These objects keep track of what function should be called and what arguments are passed to it. You can chain several delayed operations together, and Dask builds a graph of these tasks.

Execute in Parallel: When you call **compute()** on a Delayed object, Dask executes the entire graph of tasks in parallel. Dask determines the optimal order of execution and runs tasks on multiple threads or processes, handling dependencies between tasks.

```python
from dask import delayed

@delayed
def inc(x):
    return x + 1

@delayed
def add(x, y):
    return x + y

a = inc(1)
b = inc(2)
c = add(a, b)
c.compute()
```
5

```python
from dask import delayed

@delayed
def increment(x):
    return x + 1

@delayed
def double(x):
    return x * 2

@delayed
def add(x, y):
    return x + y

data = [1, 2, 3, 4, 5]
results = [add(increment(double(x)), x) for x in data]
total = delayed(sum)(results)
total.compute()   # This line triggers the actual computation
```
50

In the above examples, **inc, increment**, **double**, and **add** are lazy functions. They build up a graph of tasks to be executed, which is only computed when **total.compute()** is called. This allows Dask to efficiently parallelize the operations.

Machine Learning with Dask-ML

Machine Learning with Dask-ML in Python leverages the power of Dask to handle larger datasets and parallel computations more effectively than traditional machine learning libraries like Scikit-Learn alone. Dask-ML extends common machine learning algorithms and tools to work with Dask collections like Dask arrays and Dask DataFrames.

Here's how Dask-ML works:

Integration with Scikit-Learn: Dask-ML offers compatibility with Scikit-Learn, which means it can handle Scikit-Learn's algorithms but on larger datasets. It does this by breaking down the large dataset into smaller, manageable chunks and processing these chunks in parallel.

Handling Larger-than-memory Data: Traditional machine learning libraries often run into memory constraints when dealing with very large datasets. Dask-ML is designed to work efficiently with datasets that are larger than a machine's memory. It processes data in chunks, thereby reducing the memory requirement for each operation.

Parallel Processing: Dask-ML can distribute the computation process across multiple cores of a single machine or even across a cluster of machines. This parallel processing capability speeds up the training and prediction processes significantly, especially for large datasets.

Scalable Machine Learning Algorithms: While some algorithms in Dask-ML are direct parallels of Scikit-Learn's implementations but adapted for parallel execution, others are specifically designed for distributed environments. These include linear models, clustering, decomposition, preprocessing, and model selection.

For example, using Dask-ML for a linear regression model on a large dataset can look something like this:

```
from dask_ml.linear_model import LinearRegression
from dask_ml.datasets import make_regression

X, y = make_regression(n_samples=100000, n_features=5, chunks=500)
lr = LinearRegression()
lr.fit(X, y)
lr.predict(X)
```

In the example above, Dask-ML's **LinearRegression** is used in a similar way to Scikit-Learn's, but it's capable of handling larger datasets that wouldn't fit into memory if using standard Scikit-Learn.

Dask Distributed Client

The Dask Distributed Client is an enhanced scheduler that enables parallel and distributed computing. It's more powerful than the default scheduler and is ideal for handling complex tasks and large datasets, whether on a single machine or across a cluster.

Setup and Initialization

The Dask Distributed Client is set up by creating a **Client** object. This object manages the connection to a Dask cluster, which can be on your local machine or on a remote cluster.

This code below initializes a local Dask scheduler and workers. It automatically configures and optimizes itself for your machine.

```
from dask.distributed import Client
# Creating a local Dask cluster and connecting to it
client = Client()
```

Usage

Once the client is set up, you can use Dask as usual. The client automatically redirects computations to the distributed scheduler, which manages task execution, load balancing, and resource allocation.

```
import dask.array as da
# Creating a large random Dask array
x = da.random.random(size=(10000, 10000), chunks=(1000, 1000))

# Performing a computation
y = x + x.T
y_sum = y.sum()
result = y_sum.compute()   # This computation is handled by the distributed scheduler
print(result)
```
```
100001925.44915129
```

Monitoring and Diagnostics

The Distributed Client provides a web-based dashboard for real-time monitoring of tasks, resource usage, and other diagnostics, which is invaluable for optimizing and debugging large computations.

Persisting Data in Dask

When you persist data in Dask, it actively keeps the data in memory across the cluster's workers. This means that instead of recomputing the data each time it's needed, the precomputed results are readily available for future computations. It's particularly useful for intermediate results that are expensive to compute and are used multiple times in subsequent operations.

```python
import dask.dataframe as dd
from dask.distributed import Client

client = Client()

# Loading a large dataset into a Dask DataFrame
ddf = dd.read_csv('large_dataset.csv')

# Performing some computations
transformed_ddf = ddf.groupby(ddf.column).mean()

# Persisting the data in memory
persisted_ddf = transformed_ddf.persist()

# Future computations will be faster as they use the persisted data
result = persisted_ddf.compute()
```

In the example above, after the groupby and mean calculations, the **persist()** method is called on **transformed_ddf**. This instructs Dask to keep the resulting DataFrame in memory across the cluster's workers. Any subsequent computations using **persisted_ddf** will be faster, as they don't need to recompute the intermediate results.

CHAPTER 5: MATPLOTLIB - DATA VISUALIZATION

Introduction to Matplotlib

Matplotlib is the foundational library of the Python data visualization stack. It provides an object-oriented API for embedding plots into applications using general-purpose GUI toolkits like Tkinter, Python, Qt, or GTK. Its pyplot module is reminiscent of MATLAB, and it offers a procedural interface to the Matplotlib object-oriented plotting library. Matplotlib is highly customizable and capable of producing publication-quality plots with just a few lines of code for various formats, from histograms to scatter plots.

Installation

pip install matplotlib

Basic Plots and Customizations

Matplotlib is versatile, allowing users to create a wide range of plots and charts. Basic plots include line plots, scatter plots, bar charts, and histograms. Customizing these plots can involve adding titles, labels, adjusting colors, setting line styles and markers, and adding a legend.

For example, creating a simple line plot can be done with the following code:

```python
import matplotlib.pyplot as plt

x = [1, 2, 3, 4]
y = [10, 20, 25, 30]

plt.plot(x, y)
plt.title('Example Line Plot')
plt.xlabel('X Axis Label')
plt.ylabel('Y Axis Label')
plt.show()
```

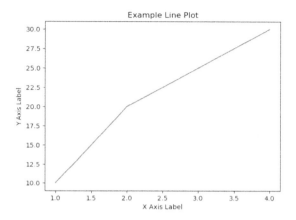

Line Plots

Pandas integration with Matplotlib simplifies the visualization of data directly from DataFrames and Series. By calling the **plot()** method on Pandas data structures, you can generate a plot with a syntax that is much simpler and more intuitive for those already familiar with Pandas.

Here's a quick example of plotting from a Pandas DataFrame:

```
df = pd.DataFrame({
    'x': [1, 2, 3, 4],
    'y': [10, 20, 25, 30]
})
df.plot('x', 'y')
```

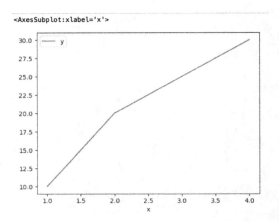

`<AxesSubplot:xlabel='x'>`

Scatterplots

```
import matplotlib.pyplot as plt
# Sample data
x = [5, 7, 8, 7, 2, 17, 2, 9, 4, 11, 12, 9, 6]
y = [99, 86, 87, 88, 100, 86, 103, 87, 94, 78, 77, 85, 86]
plt.scatter(x, y)

plt.title('Sample Scatter Plot')
plt.xlabel('X-axis Label')
plt.ylabel('Y-axis Label')

# Show the plot
plt.show()
```

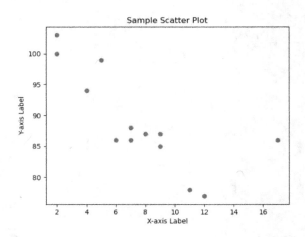

Bar Chart

```python
import matplotlib.pyplot as plt

# Sample data
x = ['Label1', 'Label2', 'Label3', 'Label4', 'Label5']
y = [1, 3, 2, 5, 4]

plt.bar(x, y)  # Creating a bar plot

# Rotate labels on the x-axis
plt.xticks(rotation=45)  # Rotates x-axis labels by 45 degrees

plt.title('Sample Bar Plot with Rotated Labels')
plt.xlabel('Categories')
plt.ylabel('Values')

# Show the plot
plt.show()
```

The resulting bar plot is shown below, also, you will observe that the labels are rotated. The above code shows how you can rotate labels in matplotlib.

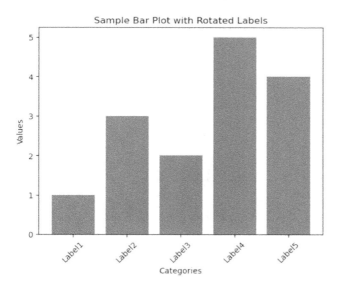

Advanced Plots and Techniques

Matplotlib also supports a variety of advanced plots such as stacked bar charts, pie charts, error bars, box plots, and contour plots. It can handle the creation of 3D plots and the customization of tick marks, gridlines, and other plot elements.

Creating a more complex plot, like a histogram, with customizations might look like this:

```
data = np.random.normal(0, 1, 1000)

plt.hist(data, bins=30, alpha=0.5, color='black', edgecolor='black')
plt.title('Histogram')
plt.xlabel('Value')
plt.ylabel('Frequency')
plt.grid(True)
plt.show()
```

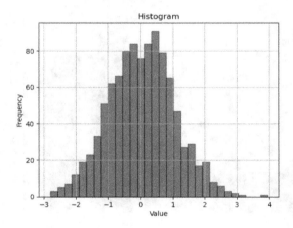

3D Plots

For 3D plotting, you would use Matplotlib's **mplot3d** toolkit:

```python
from mpl_toolkits.mplot3d import Axes3D

fig = plt.figure()
ax = fig.add_subplot(111, projection='3d')

x = [1, 2, 3, 4]
y = [10, 20, 25, 30]
z = [5, 10, 15, 20]

ax.scatter(x, y, z)
ax.set_xlabel('X Label')
ax.set_ylabel('Y Label')
ax.set_zlabel('Z Label')
plt.show()
```

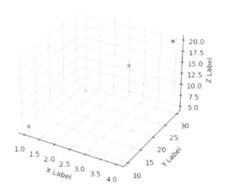

Pie Charts

Pie Chart is usually plotted with matplotlib.

```python
import matplotlib.pyplot as plt

# Pie chart, where the slices will be ordered and plotted counter-clockwise:
labels = 'Frogs', 'Hogs', 'Dogs', 'Logs'
sizes = [15, 30, 45, 10]  # The percentage of each slice
explode = (0, 0.1, 0, 0)  # Only "explode" the 2nd slice (i.e. 'Hogs')

fig1, ax1 = plt.subplots()
ax1.pie(sizes, explode=explode, labels=labels, autopct='%1.1f%%',
        shadow=True, startangle=90)
ax1.axis('equal')  # Equal aspect ratio ensures that pie is drawn as a circle.

plt.show()
```

- **labels** defines the names of the categories.

- **sizes** is a list of the values associated with each category.

- **explode** can be used to offset a slice of the pie chart.

- **autopct** is a string used to label the wedges with their numeric value.

- The format string will be fmt%pct.

- **shadow** adds a shadow to the pie chart for a 3D effect.

- **startangle** rotates the start of the pie chart by angle degrees counterclockwise from the x-axis.

- **ax1.axis('equal')** ensures the pie chart is drawn as a circle, otherwise, it would be an oval.

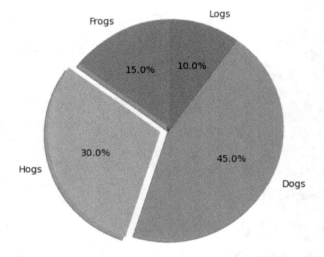

Subplots

Creating subplots involves arranging multiple plots in a grid within a single figure. The following is an example of subplots in matplotlib.

```
import matplotlib.pyplot as plt
import numpy as np
# Sample data
x = np.linspace(0, 2*np.pi, 400)
y = np.sin(x**2)

# Create a 2x2 grid of subplots
fig, axs = plt.subplots(2, 2)

# Top-left subplot
axs[0, 0].plot(x, y)
axs[0, 0].set_title('Axis [0, 0]')

# Top-right subplot
axs[0, 1].plot(x, y, 'tab:orange')
axs[0, 1].set_title('Axis [0, 1]')

# Bottom-left subplot
axs[1, 0].plot(x, -y, 'tab:green')
axs[1, 0].set_title('Axis [1, 0]')

# Bottom-right subplot
axs[1, 1].plot(x, -y, 'tab:red')
axs[1, 1].set_title('Axis [1, 1]')

# Adjust layout
plt.tight_layout()

# Show plot
plt.show()
```

plt.subplots(2, 2) creates a figure and a 2x2 grid of axes (subplots), returning a figure object (**fig**) and an array of axes objects (**axs**).

Each subplot (**axs[i, j]**) can be accessed and modified individually, where **i** is the row index and **j** is the column index.

We plot different variations of our **x** and **y** data on each subplot and set individual titles.

plt.tight_layout() adjusts the spacing between subplots for a cleaner look.

plt.show() displays the final figure with all the subplots.

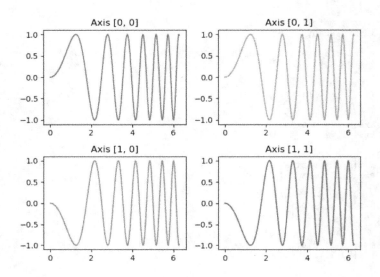

Saving Figure

After you have created your plot, you can save it to a file using the **savefig()**
method. Here's how to do it:

```python
import matplotlib.pyplot as plt

# Sample data
x = [0, 1, 2, 3, 4]
y = [0, 1, 4, 9, 16]

plt.plot(x, y)
plt.title("Sample Plot")
plt.xlabel("x")
plt.ylabel("y")
plt.savefig('sample_plot.png')  # Saves the plot as a PNG file
plt.show()
```

The figure plotted above will be saved as sample_plot.png in the working
directory. You can specify the directory and file name if you want a specified
folder.

The **savefig()** function offers several parameters to customize the saved
figure:

<u>Filename and Format</u>: You can specify the filename and format (like PNG, PDF, SVG).

plt.savefig('sample_plot.svg') # Saves the plot as an SVG file

<u>Resolution (DPI)</u>: Set the resolution of the figure in dots-per-inch.

plt.savefig('high_res_plot.png', dpi=300) # High resolution

<u>Quality</u>: Particularly for JPEG format, you can adjust the quality.

plt.savefig('sample_plot.jpg', quality=95)

<u>Transparency</u>: You can save figures with a transparent background.

plt.savefig('transparent_plot.png', transparent=True)

<u>Bounding Box</u>: Adjust the bounding box of the figure.

plt.savefig('tight_layout_plot.png', bbox_inches='tight')

Customizing Fonts, Titles, and Figure Aesthetics

While Matplotlib defaults often suffice for quick visualizations, the library's true power lies in its customization capabilities. Adjusting fonts, titles, figure sizes, and overall aesthetics can turn a simple plot into a polished figure suitable for any professional report or presentation.

To customize the font properties of your plots, you can use the **fontdict** parameter in functions like **title()**, **xlabel()**, and **ylabel()**. Additionally, you can set a global font size or style using **rcParams** to ensure consistency across your figures.

Here is how you can change the font size, weight, and style for a plot title:

plt.title('My Plot Title', fontdict={'fontsize': 18, 'fontweight': 'bold', 'color': 'green'})

For adjusting the font of tick labels, you can use the **tick_params** method:

```
plt.tick_params(axis='both', which='major', labelsize=14)
```

The size of the figure is set when you first create the figure using the **figure()** function. You can specify the width and height in inches like so:

```
plt.figure(figsize=(8, 6))
```

The figure's resolution (dots per inch) can also be set using the **dpi** parameter, which is especially useful when saving figures to files:

```
plt.figure(dpi=300)
```

When saving figures, you might want to adjust the format, quality, and resolution. The **savefig()** function allows for detailed customization:

```
plt.savefig('my_figure.png', format='png', dpi=1200, quality=95)
```

Finally, Matplotlib's style sheets allow for the easy customization of multiple plot properties. You can choose from a variety of pre-defined styles or define your own:

```
plt.style.use('ggplot')
```

Or, to temporarily use a style for a specific block of code:

```
with plt.style.context('dark_background'):
        plt.plot(x, y)
        plt.show()
```

CHAPTER 6: SEABORN - STATISTICAL DATA VISUALIZATION

Introduction to Seaborn

Seaborn is a Python data visualization library based on Matplotlib that provides a high-level interface for drawing attractive and informative statistical graphics. It is particularly suited for visualizing complex data from multi-dimensional datasets. Seaborn comes with several built-in themes and color palettes to make statistical plots more attractive and legible.

Installation

pip install seaborn

Visualization

Scatter Plot: This plot shows the relationship between two variables. Seaborn's **scatterplot** function makes it easy to draw a scatter plot and can be enhanced by mapping additional variables to color, size, and style.

```
sns.scatterplot(data=df, x="variable_x", y="variable_y", hue="category")
```

Line Plot: Useful for displaying data points sequentially connected by line segments. Seaborn's **lineplot** is handy for time series data.

```
sns.lineplot(data=df, x="variable_x", y="variable_y", hue="category")
```

Bar Plot: It shows the relationship between a numerical variable and one or more categorical variables using bars. Seaborn's **barplot** can also display the confidence intervals for the mean value of the numerical variable.

```
sns.barplot(data=df, x="category", y="value")
```

Heatmap: A data visualization technique that shows magnitude of a phenomenon as color in two dimensions. It is useful for cross-tabulated data.

```
sns.heatmap(data=pivot_table) #need to create a pivot table
```

Visualizing Distributions

Understanding the distribution of data is fundamental in statistics. Seaborn simplifies the process of exploring these distributions.

Let's import the data that we can use for example:

```
import pandas as pd
file_directory = r"/xxx/Books/Data Science Toolbox/Codes/BNB Historical Data - Investing.com2015_to_2022.csv"
data = pd.read_csv(file_directory)
data.head()
```

	Date	Price	Open	High	Low	Vol.	Change %
0	16-Feb-22	430.80	432.31	433.28	427.90	1.09M	-0.33%
1	15-Feb-22	432.21	403.49	441.20	402.70	1.24M	7.12%
2	14-Feb-22	403.49	397.83	404.20	390.61	500.69K	1.43%
3	13-Feb-22	397.80	403.22	407.02	394.90	426.23K	-1.34%
4	12-Feb-22	403.20	400.16	406.90	393.59	569.68K	0.75%

Note: we import the data using pandas and store it in a **DataFrame** called **data**.

Histograms can be created with the **distplot** function, which can also fit and plot a kernel density estimate (KDE).

```
import seaborn as sns
sns.distplot(data["Price"], bins=30, kde=True)
```

<AxesSubplot:xlabel='Price', ylabel='Density'>

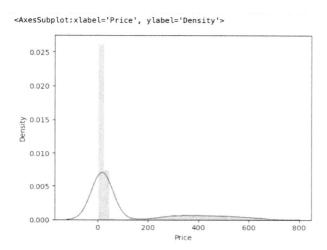

KDE plots are useful for visualizing the probability density of a continuous variable. Seaborn's **kdeplot** is a versatile function that can plot univariate or bivariate distributions.

```
sns.kdeplot(data["Price"], shade=True)
<AxesSubplot:xlabel='Price', ylabel='Density'>
```

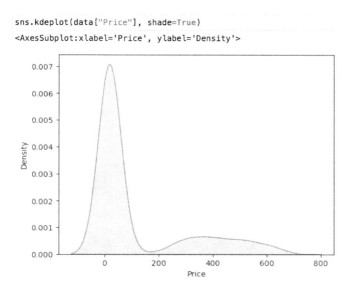

Categorical Data Plots

Seaborn shines with categorical data, offering plot types like boxplots, violin plots, and bar plots that are optimized for categorical variables.

Boxplots show the distribution of quantitative data and can be created using **boxplot**.

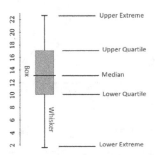

Example code:

```
sns.boxplot(x='col1', y='col2', data=df)
```

Violin plots combine boxplots with KDEs for a richer description of the data distribution.

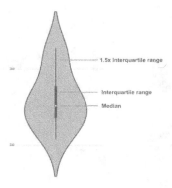

Example code:

```
sns.vioplot(x='col1', y='col2', data=df)
```

Multi-plot Grids

Seaborn makes it easy to create complex visualizations that feature multiple subplots arranged in a grid. Functions like **PairGrid** and **FacetGrid** allow for flexible creation of multi-plot grids.

PairGrid is perfect for exploring pairwise relationships in a dataset.

```
g = sns.PairGrid(data)
g.map_upper(sns.scatterplot)
g.map_lower(sns.kdeplot)
g.map_diag(sns.histplot)
```

<seaborn.axisgrid.PairGrid at 0x7fd468942df0>

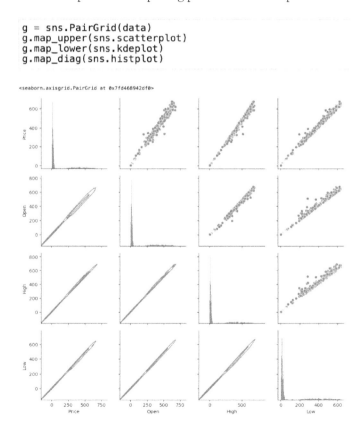

FacetGrid is used for drawing plots with multiple facets to wrap one or more axes for conditional relationships.

```
g = sns.FacetGrid(data, col='col1', row='col2')
g.map(sns.scatterplot, 'col_x', 'col_y')
```

First line creates a grid of subplots based on two categorical variables from the **data** DataFrame.

Second line plots 'col_x' and 'col_y' on the x-axis and y-axis, respectively.

Style and Theme Customization

Seaborn provides extensive support for making beautiful plots that fit the presentation or publication style you need. You can set the aesthetic parameters with functions like **set_style** and **set_palette**.

Themes can be set to control the background and gridlines.

```
sns.set_style('whitegrid')
```

Color palettes can be set to enhance the visual appeal and clarity of plots.

```
sns.set_palette('pastel')
```

CHAPTER 7: PLOTLY

Introduction to Plotly

Plotly is a versatile and interactive graphing library for Python (and other programming languages). It's widely used for creating elaborate plots, dashboards, and data visualizations in a format that's both visually appealing and user-friendly. Plotly excels in creating interactive plots that can be embedded in web applications or viewed in Jupyter notebooks.

Key Features of Plotly:

1. **Interactivity**: Offers zoom, pan, hover, and more interactive features, making it ideal for exploring complex datasets.

2. **Wide Range of Plot Types**: Supports a variety of charts including line plots, scatter plots, bar charts, pie charts, 3D charts, and geographical maps.

3. **Highly Customizable**: Provides extensive customization options for plot layout, styling, and design.

4. **Integration**: Works well with Pandas and NumPy; integrates with Dash for creating interactive web applications.

5. **Output Formats**: Can generate plots in various formats suitable for web applications or static images for reports.

Installation

pip install plotly

Visualization in Plotly

The following are examples of visualization capabilities of Plotly.

Creating a Simple Line Plot

Here's how you can create a basic line plot with Plotly.

```python
import plotly.graph_objs as go

# Sample data
x = [1, 2, 3, 4, 5]
y = [10, 11, 12, 13, 14]

# Create a trace
trace = go.Scatter(
    x = x,
    y = y,
    mode = 'lines+markers',
    name = 'Line plot'
)

# Create a layout
layout = go.Layout(title='Simple Line Plot')

# Create a figure and add trace and layout
fig = go.Figure(data=[trace], layout=layout)

# Show plot
fig.show()
```

Simple Line Plot

Creating a Bar Chart

This example demonstrates how to create an interactive bar chart.

```python
import plotly.graph_objs as go

# Data
data = [go.Bar(
        x=['Apples', 'Oranges', 'Bananas'],
        y=[20, 14, 23]
)]

# Layout
layout = go.Layout(title='Fruit Sales')

# Figure
fig = go.Figure(data=data, layout=layout)

# Show plot
fig.show()
```

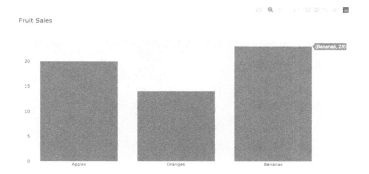

Fruit Sales

Interactive Scatter Plot

An example of creating an interactive scatter plot.

```python
import plotly.express as px

# Sample Data
df = px.data.iris()  # Iris dataset

# Scatter Plot
fig = px.scatter(df, x="sepal_width", y="sepal_length", color="species",
                 size='petal_length', hover_data=['petal_width'])

# Show plot
fig.show()
```

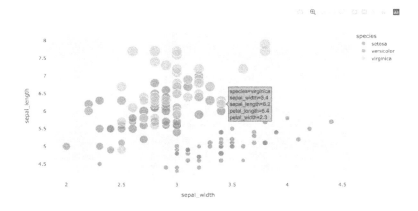

3D Plots

Plotly can create interactive 3D plots, which are particularly useful for exploring complex datasets.

```python
import plotly.graph_objects as go
import numpy as np

# Sample 3D data
z_data = np.random.poisson(5, (32, 32))

fig = go.Figure(data=[go.Surface(z=z_data)])
fig.update_layout(title='3D Surface Plot', autosize=False)
fig.show()
```

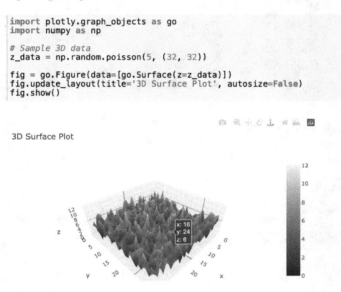

3D Surface Plot

Subplots

Create figures with multiple subplots of different types.

```python
from plotly.subplots import make_subplots
import plotly.graph_objects as go

fig = make_subplots(rows=1, cols=2)
fig.add_trace(go.Scatter(y=[4, 2, 1]), row=1, col=1)
fig.add_trace(go.Bar(y=[2, 1, 3]), row=1, col=2)
fig.show()
```

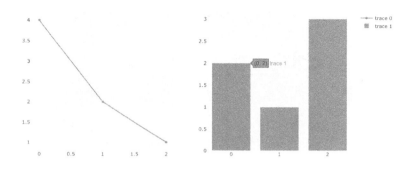

Time Series Analysis

Plotly is excellent for visualizing time series data.

```
import plotly.express as px
df = px.data.stocks()
fig = px.line(df, x='date', y="GOOG", title='Google Stock Prices')
fig.show()
```

Google Stock Prices

Interactive Maps

Create interactive geographical maps.

```python
import plotly.express as px

df = px.data.gapminder().query("year==2007")
fig = px.scatter_geo(df, locations="iso_alpha", color="continent",
                     hover_name="country", size="pop",
                     projection="natural earth")
fig.show()
```

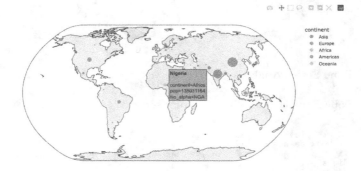

Animations

Generate animations to show data changes over time or to highlight transitions.

```python
import plotly.express as px
df = px.data.gapminder()
fig = px.scatter(df, x="gdpPercap", y="lifeExp", animation_frame="year",
                 animation_group="country", size="pop", color="continent")
fig.show()
```

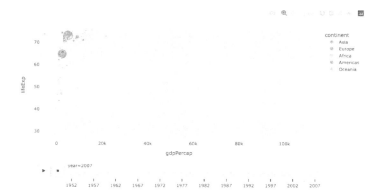

Financial Charts

Specialized plots like candlestick and time-series charts for financial analysis.

```
import plotly.graph_objects as go
df = px.data.stocks(indexed=True)-1
fig = go.Figure(data=[go.Candlestick(x=df.index, open=df['GOOG'], high=df['GOOG'], low=df['GOOG'],
                                     close=df['AAPL'])])
fig.show()
```

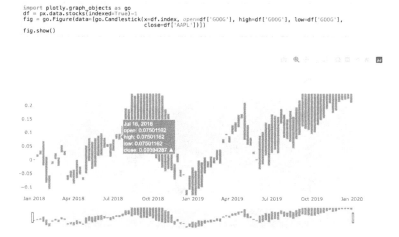

By adjusting the scale below the plot, we obtain:

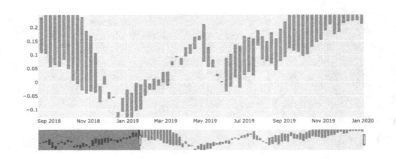

Heatmaps and Contour Plots

Useful for representing data density or intensity of variables, correlation matrices, etc.

```python
import plotly.express as px
fig = px.density_heatmap(px.data.tips(), x="total_bill", y="tip")
fig.show()
```

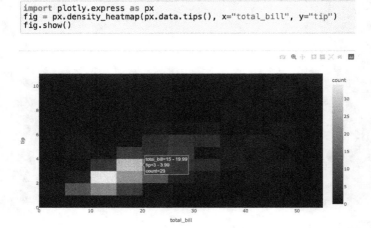

CHAPTER 8: MACHINE LEARNING WITH SCIKIT LEARN

Introduction to Scikit Learn

Scikit-Learn is a robust and widely used machine learning library in Python, offering a variety of tools for data analysis and modeling. It is known for its simplicity, efficiency, and broad compatibility with numerous Python libraries.

Data Preprocessing

Key Steps in Data Preprocessing include:

Data Cleaning

Handling Missing Data: Data often has missing values. These can be handled by filling them with a placeholder value (like the mean or median), or sometimes by dropping the rows or columns containing them.

Filling missing values using Pandas

```
import pandas as pd
df['column'].fillna(df['column'].mean(), inplace=True)   # Replace NaNs with mean
```

Removing Noise: Smoothing noisy data, typically through techniques like rolling mean, binning, clustering, or regression.

Using a simple filter to smooth data.

```
rolling_mean = df['column'].rolling(window=5).mean()   # Smooth with a rolling mean
```

Correcting Inconsistencies: Identifying and fixing errors in the data, such as typos or mislabeled classes.

Identifying and fixing errors.

```
df['column'] = df['column'].replace(['error_value'], 'correct_value')
```

Data Transformation

Normalization: Scaling the data so that it fits within a specific scale, like 0–1 or -1–1. This is important for algorithms that are sensitive to the scale of data, such as neural networks.

Scaling data to a [0, 1] range with Scikit-Learn.

```
from sklearn.preprocessing import MinMaxScaler
scaler = MinMaxScaler()
df['normalized'] = scaler.fit_transform(df[['column']])
```

Standardization: Transforming data so that it has a mean of 0 and a standard deviation of 1. This is useful for algorithms that assume the data is centered around zero.

Standardizing data to have a mean=0 and variance=1.

```
from sklearn.preprocessing import StandardScaler
scaler = StandardScaler()
df['standardized'] = scaler.fit_transform(df[['column']])
```

Feature Scaling: Altering the scale of features to a uniform range or distribution.

Data Reduction

Dimensionality Reduction: Reducing the number of random variables to consider, through methods like Principal Component Analysis (PCA).

Applying PCA for dimensionality reduction.

```
from sklearn.decomposition import PCA
pca = PCA(n_components=2)
reduced_data = pca.fit_transform(df)
```

Feature Selection: Identifying and selecting the most relevant features to the problem to improve model efficiency and effectiveness.

Selecting features with high correlation.

```
corr_matrix = df.corr().abs()
high_corr_var = np.where(corr_matrix > 0.8)
high_corr_var = [(corr_matrix.columns[x], corr_matrix.columns[y])
                 for x, y in zip(*high_corr_var) if x != y and x < y]
```

Data Discretization

Transforming continuous data into discrete bins. This can be useful for simplifying complex continuous features or making the data more interpretable.

Binning Data: Converting numerical data into categorical bins.

```
df['binned'] = pd.cut(df['numerical_column'], bins=[0, 10, 20, 30], labels=["Low", "Medium", "High"])
```

Encoding Categorical Data

Label Encoding: Converting each value of a categorical feature into a numerical value.

Converting categories to integers.

```
from sklearn.preprocessing import LabelEncoder
le = LabelEncoder()
df['encoded'] = le.fit_transform(df['category_column'])
```

One-Hot Encoding: Creating a binary column for each category in the original feature.

Creating binary columns for each category.

```
encoded_df = pd.get_dummies(df, columns=['categorical_column'])
```

Handling Imbalanced Data

Techniques like oversampling the minority class, undersampling the majority class, or generating synthetic samples can be used to balance the dataset.

Oversampling Minority Class: Using SMOTE for oversampling.

```
from imblearn.over_sampling import SMOTE
smote = SMOTE()
X_resampled, y_resampled = smote.fit_resample(X, y)
```

Supervised Learning

Supervised learning is a type of machine learning where the model is trained on a labeled dataset. In this context, "labeled" means that each example in the training dataset is paired with the correct output. The goal of supervised learning is for the model to learn a mapping from inputs to outputs, enabling it to predict the output for new, unseen inputs.

For instance, In a supervised learning scenario, you might have a dataset of photos of fruits, where each photo is labeled with the type of fruit it depicts (like apple, banana, cherry). The model learns to associate specific features in the photos (shape, color, texture) with each fruit type. After training, you can present the model with a new photo of a fruit, and it will predict the fruit type in the photo.

Key Characteristics of Supervised Learning

1. **Labeled Data**: The training data includes both input features (like images, text, or numerical data) and their corresponding output labels (like categories or numerical values).

2. **Training Process**: During training, the model makes predictions on the training data and is corrected when its predictions are wrong. Over time, the model "learns" to map inputs to outputs accurately.

3. **Predictions on New Data**: Once trained, the model can be used to make predictions on new, unseen data. The effectiveness of these predictions depends on the quality and representativeness of the training data.

4. **Applications**: Supervised learning is used in a variety of applications, such as image and speech recognition, spam detection, medical diagnosis, and stock price prediction.

Types of Supervised Learning

- **Classification**: The output is categorical. The goal is to categorize inputs into classes. For example, an email spam filter is a classifier that categorizes emails as 'spam' or 'not spam.'

- **Regression**: The output is continuous. The task involves predicting a numerical value. For instance, predicting house prices based on features like size and location.

Supervised Learning Algorithms

Implement various regression and classification algorithms, such Linear Regression, Logistic Regression, Decision Trees, Random Forests, Support Vector Machines (SVMs), Naive Bayes, K-Nearest Neighbors (KNN), and Gradient Boosting Machines (GBM).

```python
from sklearn.ensemble import RandomForestClassifier

clf = RandomForestClassifier()
clf.fit(X_train, y_train)
y_pred = clf.predict(X_test)
```

```
from sklearn.linear_model import LogisticRegression

model = LogisticRegression()
model.fit(X_train, y_train)
y_pred = model.predict(X_test)
```

```
from sklearn.svm import SVC

model = SVC()
model.fit(X_train, y_train)
y_pred = model.predict(X_test)
```

```
from sklearn.tree import DecisionTreeClassifier

model = DecisionTreeClassifier()
model.fit(X_train, y_train)
y_pred = model.predict(X_test)
```

```
from sklearn.linear_model import LinearRegression

model = LinearRegression()
model.fit(X_train, y_train)
y_pred = model.predict(X_test)
```

```
from sklearn.linear_model import Ridge

model = Ridge(alpha=1.0)
model.fit(X_train, y_train)
y_pred = model.predict(X_test)
```

Unsupervised Learning

Unsupervised learning is a type of machine learning that deals with unlabeled data. The key objective is to explore and find structure within this data. Unlike supervised learning, unsupervised learning algorithms are not provided with correct answers or labels. Instead, they are tasked with identifying patterns, groupings, or features in the data on their own.

For instance, consider an online retail dataset containing customer purchase histories. An unsupervised learning algorithm can be applied to segment customers into distinct groups based on purchasing patterns without any prior labeling. This segmentation could reveal groups like "frequent buyers," "seasonal shoppers," or "one-time buyers," which can then be used for targeted marketing strategies.

Key Characteristics of Unsupervised Learning:

1. **No Labeled Data**: The training data consists only of input features without any corresponding target values or labels.

2. **Discovery of Hidden Patterns**: Unsupervised learning algorithms seek to find structure in the data, such as grouping similar data points together (clustering) or discovering the underlying distribution (density estimation).

3. **Data Exploration**: It is often used for exploratory data analysis to find hidden patterns or groupings in data.

4. **Feature Extraction**: Unsupervised learning can be used for feature extraction, where the algorithm creates new features from the existing ones, which can then be used for further analysis or in supervised learning tasks.

Types of Unsupervised Learning:

1. **Clustering**: The most common unsupervised learning technique, clustering, is used to group data points together based on their similarity. Common algorithms include K-Means, hierarchical clustering, and DBSCAN.

2. **Dimensionality Reduction**: Techniques like Principal Component Analysis (PCA) and t-Distributed Stochastic Neighbor Embedding (t-SNE) reduce the number of variables in the dataset while preserving as much of the original data's variability as possible.

3. **Association Rule Learning**: This technique is used to discover interesting relationships between variables in large databases, commonly used in market basket analysis.

Unsupervised Learning Algorithms

Includes K-Means clustering, T-distributed Stochastic Neighbor Embedding (t-SNE), DBSCAN clustering, Agglomerative clustering, factor analysis, and principal component analysis.

```python
from sklearn.cluster import KMeans

kmeans = KMeans(n_clusters=3)
kmeans.fit(X)
labels = kmeans.predict(X)
```

```python
from sklearn.decomposition import PCA

pca = PCA(n_components=2)
X_reduced = pca.fit_transform(X)
```

```python
from sklearn.cluster import AgglomerativeClustering

clustering = AgglomerativeClustering(n_clusters=3)
labels = clustering.fit_predict(X)
```

```python
from sklearn.cluster import DBSCAN

dbscan = DBSCAN(eps=0.5, min_samples=5)
labels = dbscan.fit_predict(X)
```

```python
from sklearn.manifold import TSNE

tsne = TSNE(n_components=2, perplexity=30.0)
X_embedded = tsne.fit_transform(X)
```

Model Selection

Model selection is the process of choosing one or more models from a set of candidates based on their performance on a given task. It's not just about picking the model with the best performance on the training data, but also about finding a model that generalizes well to unseen data.

1) **Cross-Validation**: A technique for assessing how the results of a statistical analysis will generalize to an independent data set. It involves partitioning the

data into subsets, training the model on one subset, and validating it on another.

```
from sklearn.model_selection import cross_val_score
scores = cross_val_score(model, X, y, cv=5)  # 5-fold cross-validation
```

2) **Grid Search**: An exhaustive search over specified parameter values for an estimator, useful for tuning hyperparameters.

```
from sklearn.model_selection import GridSearchCV
parameters = {'kernel':('linear', 'rbf'), 'C':[1, 10]}
grid_search = GridSearchCV(estimator, parameters)
grid_search.fit(X_train, y_train)
```

Evaluation Metrics

Evaluation metrics are used to measure the performance of a model. Different problems require different metrics.

Classification Metrics

Accuracy: The ratio of correctly predicted instances to the total instances.

```
from sklearn.metrics import accuracy_score
accuracy = accuracy_score(y_true, y_pred)
```

Precision and Recall: Precision is the ratio of correctly predicted positive observations to the total predicted positives. Recall (Sensitivity) is the ratio of correctly predicted positive observations to all observations in the actual class.

```
from sklearn.metrics import precision_score, recall_score
precision = precision_score(y_true, y_pred)
recall = recall_score(y_true, y_pred)
```

F1 Score: The weighted average of Precision and Recall.

```
from sklearn.metrics import f1_score
f1 = f1_score(y_true, y_pred)
```

Regression Metrics

<u>Mean Absolute Error (MAE)</u>: The average of the absolute differences between predictions and actual values.

```python
from sklearn.metrics import mean_absolute_error
mae = mean_absolute_error(y_true, y_pred)
```

<u>Mean Squared Error (MSE)</u>: The average of the squares of the differences between predicted and actual values.

```python
from sklearn.metrics import mean_squared_error
mse = mean_squared_error(y_true, y_pred)
```

<u>R^2 Score</u>: Indicates the proportion of the variance in the dependent variable that is predictable from the independent variables.

```python
from sklearn.metrics import r2_score
r2 = r2_score(y_true, y_pred)
```

Dimensionality Reduction

Techniques to reduce the number of input variables in the dataset, such as PCA.

```python
from sklearn.decomposition import PCA

pca = PCA(n_components=2)
X_reduced = pca.fit_transform(X)
```

Pipeline Creation

Simplify the process of building a sequence of data transforms and a model.

```python
from sklearn.pipeline import make_pipeline

pipeline = make_pipeline(StandardScaler(), RandomForestClassifier())
pipeline.fit(X_train, y_train)
```

Full ML Code Example with Scikit Learn

The following is an example of a complete supervised learning workflow in Python using Scikit-Learn, including data preprocessing and model training with evaluation. In this example, let's assume we are working with a hypothetical dataset for a binary classification task, where the objective is to predict a binary outcome based on various features.

```python
# Import necessary libraries
import pandas as pd
from sklearn.model_selection import train_test_split
from sklearn.preprocessing import StandardScaler, OneHotEncoder
from sklearn.compose import ColumnTransformer
from sklearn.pipeline import Pipeline
from sklearn.impute import SimpleImputer
from sklearn.ensemble import RandomForestClassifier
from sklearn.metrics import accuracy_score

# Load dataset
data = pd.read_csv('data.csv')

# Separate features and target variable
X = data.drop('target', axis=1)
y = data['target']

# Split data into training and test sets
X_train, X_test, y_train, y_test = train_test_split(X, y, test_size=0.2, random_state=42)
```

Data Preprocessing

```python
# Numerical features to be scaled
numeric_features = ['feature1', 'feature2', 'feature3']
numeric_transformer = Pipeline(steps=[
    ('imputer', SimpleImputer(strategy='mean')),   # Handle missing values
    ('scaler', StandardScaler())])                 # Scale data

# Categorical features to be encoded
categorical_features = ['feature4', 'feature5']
categorical_transformer = Pipeline(steps=[
    ('imputer', SimpleImputer(strategy='constant', fill_value='missing')),  # Handle missing values
    ('onehot', OneHotEncoder(handle_unknown='ignore'))])                    # One-hot encode data

# Column transformer for parallel preprocessing
preprocessor = ColumnTransformer(
    transformers=[
        ('num', numeric_transformer, numeric_features),
        ('cat', categorical_transformer, categorical_features)])

# Complete pipeline with preprocessing and model training
clf = Pipeline(steps=[('preprocessor', preprocessor),
                      ('classifier', RandomForestClassifier())])
```

Model Training and Evaluation

```python
# Train the model
clf.fit(X_train, y_train)

# Predict on the test set
y_pred = clf.predict(X_test)

# Evaluate the model
accuracy = accuracy_score(y_test, y_pred)
print(f'Model Accuracy: {accuracy:.2f}')
```

CHAPTER 9: DEEP LEARNING WITH TENSORFLOW AND KERAS

Introduction

TensorFlow is an open-source machine learning library developed by Google, and Keras is a high-level neural networks API that can run on top of TensorFlow. Together, they provide a powerful toolkit for deep learning, allowing for the creation and training of complex neural network models.

Key Features of TensorFlow and Keras:

1. **Flexibility and Scalability**: TensorFlow supports a wide range of complex calculations and is scalable from small to large datasets.

2. **Keras API**: Keras provides a more user-friendly interface, simplifying many TensorFlow tasks with its high-level, Pythonic commands.

3. **GPU and TPU Support**: Accelerate computations using GPUs or TPUs to train and deploy models faster.

4. **Extensive Toolset**: Offers tools for data loading, model building, training, evaluation, and deployment.

Installation

```
pip install tensorflow #keras is integrated with tensorflow 2.x

pip install keras #if less than tensorflow 2.x
```

Creating a Simple Neural Network

Building a Sequential model for classification.

```
import tensorflow as tf
from tensorflow import keras

model = keras.Sequential([
    keras.layers.Flatten(input_shape=(28, 28)),    # Input layer
    keras.layers.Dense(128, activation='relu'),     # Hidden layer
    keras.layers.Dense(10, activation='softmax')    # Output layer
])
```

The model above represents a neural network and is structured into three key parts: the input layer, hidden layers, and the output layer. The input layer serves as the initial point where data is fed into the model. Each neuron in this layer corresponds to a distinct feature or element of the input data. The hidden layers, situated between the input and output layers, are composed of neurons that perform various computations on the inputs received. These layers are important for the network's ability to make complex associations and learn from the data, yet they are termed 'hidden' as their internal workings and transformations are not directly visible or interpretable. Finally, the output layer is responsible for producing the final result of the neural network, such as a classification or a prediction, based on the processed information from the hidden layers. This structure allows the neural network to transform input data into meaningful outputs through a series of computational steps.

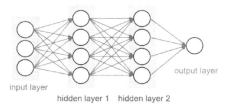

(A typical Neural Network, this does not represent the model in the code above)

Compiling the Model

This stage involves specifying key components such as, the optimizer, the loss function, and the metrics. The optimizer is an algorithm that adjusts the weights of the network to minimize errors in predictions; it essentially determines how the network updates itself based on the data it sees. Common optimizers include SGD (Stochastic Gradient Descent), Adam, and RMSprop, each having different approaches to navigating the complex landscape of weights to find the best settings. The loss function, also known as the cost function, quantifies how far off the predictions are from the actual results; it's the objective the optimizer aims to minimize. For example, 'mean squared error' is a common loss function for regression tasks. Lastly, metrics are used to evaluate the performance of the model during training and testing. These are different from the loss function in that they don't directly influence the training, but rather provide insight into how well the model is performing. Common metrics include accuracy, precision, and recall. Together, the optimizer, loss function, and metrics guide the training process to effectively learn from the data.

```
model.compile(optimizer='adam',
              loss='sparse_categorical_crossentropy',
              metrics=['accuracy'])
```

Training the Model

Training neural networks model involves iteratively processing the input data and adjusting the model's weights to improve its predictions. A key component of this process is the use of 'epochs', which are essentially the number of times the entire dataset is passed forward and backward through the neural network. Each epoch consists of a series of batches, where the network's weights are updated after processing each batch of data. The size of these batches and the number of epochs is critical parameters: larger batch sizes provide a more accurate estimate of the gradient, but require more memory and computational power, while more epochs can lead to better learning but also increase the risk of overfitting if the model starts to learn noise and inaccuracies in the data.

Other inputs might include the validation split which specifies the percentage of data that will be reserved for validation of the model after training, learning rate, which determines the step size at each iteration while moving toward a minimum of the loss function, and callbacks, which are tools for monitoring the model's performance and behavior at certain stages of training. Optimizing these parameters is essential for effective model training, striking a balance between computational efficiency and the accuracy of the learning process.

```
# Train the model
model.fit(train_images, train_labels,
                epochs=10,             # Number of epochs
                batch_size=32,         # Size of the batches of data
                validation_split=0.2)  # Percentage of data used for validation
```

Prediction and Evaluation of the Model

Evaluating a neural network model involves assessing its performance using appropriate metrics, which depend on the specific nature and objectives of the task at hand. For classification problems, common metrics include accuracy, precision, recall, and the F1 score. Accuracy is used for a general sense of model performance but might be misleading in imbalanced datasets, where precision (the proportion of true positives among positive predictions) and recall (the proportion of true positives identified correctly) provide more insights. The F1 score, which is the harmonic mean of precision and recall, offers a balance between the two, particularly in cases of uneven class distribution. For regression tasks, metrics like mean absolute error (MAE), mean squared error (MSE), or root mean squared error (RMSE) are commonly used, each quantifying the difference between predicted and actual values in different ways. Selecting the right metric is key as it guides the optimization of the model and ultimately determines how well the model performs according to the specific requirements of the given task.

```python
#Basic Metric
test_loss, test_accuracy = model.evaluate(test_images, test_labels, verbose=2)

predictions = model.predict(test_images)

#For regression model
mse = mean_squared_error(test_labels, predictions)
mae = mean_absolute_error(test_labels, predictions)

#For classification model
predictions = model.predict(test_images)
predicted_classes = np.argmax(predictions, axis=1)

print(classification_report(test_labels, predicted_classes))
```

Different Ways of Building Models

Building a model in TensorFlow and Keras can be done in various ways, catering to different levels of complexity and customization.

1. Sequential API

The Sequential API is the simplest way to build a model in Keras. It allows you to create models layer-by-layer in a step-by-step fashion. This approach is suitable for most deep learning models with a single input and output.

```python
from tensorflow.keras.models import Sequential
from tensorflow.keras.layers import Dense, Flatten

model = Sequential([
    Flatten(input_shape=(28, 28)),
    Dense(128, activation='relu'),
    Dense(10, activation='softmax')
])
```

2. Functional API

The Functional API provides more flexibility and is used for models with complex architectures. It allows you to create models with multiple inputs and outputs, shared layers, and non-linear connectivity topologies.

```python
from tensorflow.keras.layers import Input, Dense, concatenate
from tensorflow.keras.models import Model

# Define two input layers
input1 = Input(shape=(28, 28))
input2 = Input(shape=(28, 28))

# Create layers and connect them
x1 = Flatten()(input1)
x1 = Dense(64, activation='relu')(x1)

x2 = Flatten()(input2)
x2 = Dense(64, activation='relu')(x2)

# Merge inputs
merged = concatenate([x1, x2])

# Output layer
output = Dense(10, activation='softmax')(merged)

# Create the model
model = Model(inputs=[input1, input2], outputs=output)
```

3. Subclassing the Model Class

Model subclassing provides the ultimate flexibility. This approach involves defining a custom class that inherits from the **tf.keras.Model** class, where you can define your own forward pass. Use this for complex models or when you need full control over the model.

```python
from tensorflow.keras.layers import Dense, Flatten
from tensorflow.keras.models import Model

class CustomModel(Model):
    def __init__(self):
        super(CustomModel, self).__init__()
        self.flatten = Flatten()
        self.d1 = Dense(128, activation='relu')
        self.d2 = Dense(10, activation='softmax')

    def call(self, x):
        x = self.flatten(x)
        x = self.d1(x)
        return self.d2(x)

# Instantiate the model
model = CustomModel()
```

4. Using Pre-trained Models

Keras also provides a set of pre-trained models which can be used for transfer learning. These models are trained on large datasets and can be used as-is or customized for specific tasks.

```python
from tensorflow.keras.applications import VGG16

# Load VGG16 pre-trained on ImageNet data
model = VGG16(weights='imagenet')
```

Project Example for Sequential Model

This project will be a basic image classification task using the MNIST dataset, which consists of handwritten digits.

```python
import tensorflow as tf
from tensorflow.keras.models import Sequential
from tensorflow.keras.layers import Dense, Flatten
from tensorflow.keras.datasets import mnist
from tensorflow.keras.utils import to_categorical

# Load dataset
(train_images, train_labels), (test_images, test_labels) = mnist.load_data()

# Normalize the images.
train_images = train_images / 255.0
test_images = test_images / 255.0

# One-hot encode labels
train_labels = to_categorical(train_labels)
test_labels = to_categorical(test_labels)

# Build the model
model = Sequential([
    Flatten(input_shape=(28, 28)),
    Dense(128, activation='relu'),
    Dense(10, activation='softmax')
])

# Compile the model
model.compile(optimizer='adam',
              loss='categorical_crossentropy',
              metrics=['accuracy'])

# Train the model
model.fit(train_images, train_labels, epochs=5, batch_size=32)

# Evaluate the model
test_loss, test_acc = model.evaluate(test_images, test_labels, verbose=2)
print('\nTest accuracy:', test_acc)
```

Project Example for Functional API

This project will be a multi-input model that takes two different types of inputs and predicts a single output. We will simulate this with the MNIST dataset for demonstration purposes.

```python
import tensorflow as tf
from tensorflow.keras.layers import Input, Dense, Flatten, concatenate
from tensorflow.keras.models import Model
from tensorflow.keras.datasets import mnist
from tensorflow.keras.utils import to_categorical

# Load dataset
(train_images, train_labels), (test_images, test_labels) = mnist.load_data()

# Normalize the images.
train_images = train_images / 255.0
test_images = test_images / 255.0

# One-hot encode labels
train_labels = to_categorical(train_labels)
test_labels = to_categorical(test_labels)

# Define two input layers
input1 = Input(shape=(28, 28))
input2 = Input(shape=(28, 28))

# First branch
x1 = Flatten()(input1)
x1 = Dense(64, activation='relu')(x1)

# Second branch
x2 = Flatten()(input2)
x2 = Dense(64, activation='relu')(x2)

# Merge branches
merged = concatenate([x1, x2])

# Output layer
output = Dense(10, activation='softmax')(merged)

# Create the model
model = Model(inputs=[input1, input2], outputs=output)

# Compile the model
model.compile(optimizer='adam',
              loss='categorical_crossentropy',
              metrics=['accuracy'])

# Train the model
model.fit([train_images, train_images], train_labels, epochs=5, batch_size=32)

# Evaluate the model
test_loss, test_acc = model.evaluate([test_images, test_images], test_labels, verbose=2)
print('\nTest accuracy:', test_acc)
```

The model architecture is designed to handle dual inputs using two separate branches, each processing one input stream. The first and second branches consist of Flatten and Dense layers, independently processing two sets of identical MNIST images. After each branch independently learns from its respective input, their outputs are merged using the **concatenate** function.

This merging creates a unified representation that combines features learned from both input streams. The merged output is then fed into a final Dense layer for classification. This multi-input architecture is particularly useful for scenarios where the model needs to learn from and make decisions based on multiple distinct data sources.

CHAPTER 10: STATISTICAL ANALYSIS (INTRODUCTION)

Overview

Statistical analysis is a fundamental aspect of data science that deals with the collection, summarization, interpretation, and presentation of data. It forms the backbone of data exploration, providing the necessary tools and techniques to uncover patterns, trends, and relationships within data. The goal of statistical analysis is to convert raw data into meaningful information, which can then be used to make informed decisions and predictions. This involves various techniques ranging from basic descriptive statistics to more complex inferential methods, each serving a specific purpose in the data analysis process.

Descriptive Statistics

Descriptive statistics are used to describe and summarize data in a in a way that makes the data meaningful. They provide a simple overview of the sample and the measures. Key concepts include:

Measures of Central Tendency: These are metrics that describe the center of a dataset. The most common measures are:

- **Mean**: The average of all data points.

- **Median**: The middle value in a sorted list of numbers.

- **Mode**: The most frequently occurring value in a dataset.

Measures of Dispersion: These measures describe the spread of the data. They include:

- **Range**: The difference between the highest and lowest values.

- **Variance**: The average of the squared differences from the Mean.

- **Standard Deviation**: A measure of the amount of variation or dispersion in a set of values.

Using Python libraries such as Pandas and NumPy, we can easily compute these descriptive statistics:

```python
import pandas as pd
import numpy as np

# Example dataset
data = np.array([23, 76, 97, 28, 10, 8, 50, 100, 54, 34, 76, 82, 92, 19, 76])

# Creating a Pandas DataFrame
df = pd.DataFrame(data, columns=['Sample Data'])

# Calculating Measures of Central Tendency
mean = df['Sample Data'].mean()
median = df['Sample Data'].median()
mode = df['Sample Data'].mode()

# Calculating Measures of Dispersion
range = df['Sample Data'].max() - df['Sample Data'].min()
variance = df['Sample Data'].var()
std_deviation = df['Sample Data'].std()

# Display the results
print(f"Mean: {mean}, \n Median: {median}, \n Mode: {mode[0]}")
print(f"Range: {range}, \n Variance: {variance}, \n Standard Deviation: {std_deviation}")
```

```
Mean: 55.0,
 Median: 54.0,
 Mode: 76
Range: 92,
 Variance: 1068.5714285714287,
 Standard Deviation: 32.689010822773895
```

Probability Distributions

Probability distributions are fundamental in statistics and data science, as they describe the likelihood of different outcomes. In data analysis, understanding these distributions helps in making predictions about future events and in interpreting the data.

Probability Theory involves understanding how probabilities are measured and how they describe the likelihood of different outcomes. Probability distributions can be discrete (like a binomial distribution) or continuous (like a normal distribution).

Common Distributions

- <u>Normal Distribution:</u> Often called the bell curve, it describes a distribution where most observations cluster around the central peak and probabilities for values further away from the mean taper off equally in both directions.

- <u>Binomial Distribution</u>: Used for binary outcomes (success/failure) and described by the number of successes in a set number of trials.

- <u>Poisson Distribution</u>: Useful for counting the number of times an event occurs in a fixed interval of time or space.

- <u>Other Distributions</u>: There are many other distributions like the uniform, exponential, and gamma distributions, each with their specific applications.

Application in Python: Use of libraries like SciPy and NumPy to work with these distributions.

```python
import numpy as np
import matplotlib.pyplot as plt
from scipy.stats import norm, binom, poisson

# Example: plotting a normal distribution
data = np.arange(-5, 5, 0.1)
plt.plot(data, norm.pdf(data, 0, 1))
plt.title("Normal Distribution")
plt.show()
```

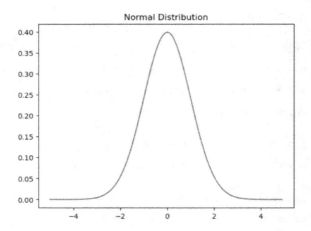

Hypothesis Testing

Hypothesis testing is a statistical method that allows you to test assumptions (hypotheses) about a parameter of the population. In hypothesis testing, two opposing hypotheses are formulated:

Null Hypothesis (H0): This is a statement of no effect or no difference, serving as the default assumption. It posits that any observed effect in the data is due to chance.

Alternative Hypothesis (H1 or Ha): Contrary to the null, this hypothesis suggests there is an effect or a difference. It's what the researcher aims to support.

P-Values are necessary in deciding between these hypotheses. A p-value represents the probability of observing the data, or something more extreme, under the assumption that the null hypothesis is true. In essence, it tells how compatible your data is with the null hypothesis. A low p-value (typically less than 0.05) indicates that the observed data is unlikely under the null hypothesis, leading to its rejection in favor of the alternative hypothesis.

Errors in hypothesis testing fall into two categories:

Type I Error: Occurs when the null hypothesis is true but is incorrectly rejected. It's akin to a false alarm.

Type II Error: Happens when the null hypothesis is false, but the test fails to reject it. This is similar to a missed detection.

Statistical Testing

In statistical analysis, different tests are employed to compare groups and make inferences. These tests are fundamental in hypothesis testing, allowing researchers to make informed conclusions about the relationships and differences between groups in their data. Some of the tests include:

T-test: This test is used when comparing the means of two groups to determine if they are statistically different from each other. There are two main types: the independent t-test for comparing two different groups and the paired t-test for comparing the same group at different times or under different conditions.

Chi-Square Tests: These tests are used primarily with categorical data. A common application is to test the hypothesis about the distribution of frequency counts among different categories. For instance, it can help determine if the distribution of some observed frequencies over different categories deviates significantly from a distribution expected under some null hypothesis.

ANOVA (Analysis of Variance): ANOVA is a method used to compare the means of more than two groups. It tests the hypothesis that each group's mean is the same. If the ANOVA returns a statistically significant result, it suggests that at least one group mean is different. Further, post-hoc tests can be conducted to identify exactly which groups differ from each other.

Interpreting Test Results

Understanding test results is important for making conclusions in data analysis. The results of hypothesis tests, in conjunction with p-values, help in determining whether to reject the null hypothesis or not. It's also important to consider the practical significance of the results, not just the statistical significance.

In the example below, a t-test is used to compare the means of two different groups. The p-value helps in determining whether the differences in the group means are statistically significant.

```
from scipy import stats

# Example: performing a t-test
group1 = [20, 21, 22, 23, 22]
group2 = [28, 31, 22, 24, 25]
t_statistic, p_value = stats.ttest_ind(group1, group2)

print("T-statistic:", t_statistic)
print("P-value:", p_value)
```

```
T-statistic: -2.6484887678869216
P-value: 0.029324480304741857
```

Inferential Statistics

From Samples to Population: Inferential statistics involves making inferences about a larger population based on sample data. It allows us to draw conclusions and make predictions about a population's characteristics by analyzing a representative sample. This process is necessary because, in many cases, it's impractical or impossible to collect data from every individual in a population.

Confidence Intervals

Confidence intervals provide a range of values within which we can expect a population parameter to lie, based on sample data. They offer a measure of the reliability of an estimated range and are key in both expressing the accuracy of sample statistics and guiding decision-making processes.

Demonstration in Python

Python's Scipy and Statsmodels libraries are powerful tools for applying inferential statistics:

```python
import scipy.stats as stats
import numpy as np

# Sample data
data = np.random.normal(loc=0, scale=1, size=30)

# Calculate a 95% confidence interval
ci = stats.norm.interval(0.95, np.mean(data), np.std(data, ddof=1))
print("Confidence Interval:", ci)

Confidence Interval: (-2.1361372443562443, 2.1299401677987033)
```

Regression Analysis

Linear regression is a foundational statistical method used in predicting outcomes. It explores the relationship between a dependent variable and one or more independent variables using a linear equation.

Implementing Regression in Python

Python's Scikit-Learn library simplifies the implementation of regression analysis:

```
from sklearn.linear_model import LinearRegression
from sklearn.model_selection import train_test_split

# Assume X and y are your features and target variable
X_train, X_test, y_train, y_test = train_test_split(X, y, test_size=0.3)

model = LinearRegression()
model.fit(X_train, y_train)
```

Note, X represents the features while y represents the target in the dataset. These variables must be defined before the split method is implemented.

Correlation vs Causation

It is essential to differentiate between correlation and causation. Correlation refers to a relationship or association between two variables, where changes in one variable mirror changes in the other. However, this does not imply that one variable causes the change in the other, which is what causation signifies. A classic example is the correlation between ice cream sales and drowning incidents; they both increase during summer, but one does not cause the other. Misinterpreting correlation for causation can lead to erroneous conclusions and faulty decision-making.

CHAPTER 11: DATA SCIENCE PROJECT LIFE CYCLE

The data science lifecycle represents a series of iterative steps undertaken to build, deliver, and maintain data science products. It's important to note that not all data science projects are identical; thus, their respective lifecycles can vary. Despite these variations, a generalized lifecycle encompasses common steps that integrates machine learning algorithms and statistical practices to develop robust prediction models. Key steps in this process include data collection, cleaning, analysis, model building, evaluation, deployment, maintenance, and optimization.

Understanding Project Scope

In the data science project lifecycle, the first critical step is understanding the project scope, which hinges on defining and analyzing the business problem to be solved. This involves transforming complex business needs into clear, actionable data science questions. Engaging with key stakeholders affected by these issues is essential, as their insights help shape the direction of the project and ensure that the data science solutions are aligned with the business objectives.

It's important to recognize that not every business challenge is suited for a data science approach. Therefore, accurately identifying and framing problems within the realm of data science significantly increases the chances of developing impactful, data-driven solutions that can transform and enhance existing business operations, be it through process optimization, improved customer satisfaction, or increased sales.

Data Collection

After defining the project scope, the next critical step is data collection. The success of a data science project heavily relies on the quality and relevance of the data collected. In many cases, organizations struggle with gathering reliable and comprehensive data, and some are even unsure about the type of data they need or where to find it.

The data collection process should be tailored to the specific business problem. For example, in customer credit risk analysis, relevant data might include demographics, loan details, repayment history, and transaction records. Using inappropriate data, like customer physical attributes for this analysis, would be irrelevant and unhelpful.

Thanks to modern technologies like web scraping, cloud data collection tools, APIs, and various database systems (MongoDB, PostgreSQL, MySQL), alongside tools like SQL, Python, R, Beautiful Soup, Scrapy, and Spark, valuable data can be extracted efficiently and effectively from a wide range of sources.

Data Cleaning

Once the data is collected, the next vital step is data cleaning and processing. Raw data is often unstructured, irrelevant, and unfiltered, making it unsuitable for direct use in model building. Without proper cleaning and processing, any analysis performed is likely to be flawed, leading to inaccurate models.

Data cleaning challenges include dealing with duplicate and null values, inconsistent data types, missing data, invalid entries, and improper formatting. These issues must be addressed to ensure the integrity and reliability of the data.

It's a well-known fact in the data science community that a significant portion of a data scientist's time is spent on data collection, cleaning, and processing, sometimes as much as 80% of the total project time. Although data cleaning can be a painstaking and time-consuming process, it is a critical step that cannot be overlooked. The quality of the data directly impacts the effectiveness of the final model.

Exploratory Data Analysis (EDA)

After cleaning and organizing the data, the next key step is Exploratory Data Analysis (EDA). This phase is all about deeply inspecting the data features and properties, building confidence in the data, and gaining intuitive insights. EDA is a fundamental process in data science, encompassing various analytical techniques such as univariate and bivariate analysis, missing values treatment, outlier treatment, variable transformation, feature engineering, and correlation analysis. Effective EDA lays the foundation for creating predictive and stable features from the original dataset.

One of the key benefits of EDA is that it allows you to ask various questions of the data, explore and visualize different datasets to identify patterns, and uncover insights that are important for the subsequent steps in the machine learning lifecycle. It also fosters innovative and analytical thinking, essential for successful data analysis.

Model Development

The model development phase is where the actual modeling of the data takes place. This stage is often seen as where the "real magic" of data science happens. The first task is to split the cleaned dataset into train and test sets. The training set is used to build predictive models, while the test set helps evaluate the model's performance on unseen data points.

Machine learning problems are generally classified into two categories: supervised and unsupervised learning. Supervised learning involves building a model to predict a target variable using known predictors, while unsupervised learning is about finding patterns and relationships among predictors without any prior labeling. The approach chosen depends on the nature of the problem and the data available.

Evaluation

Evaluating the model's performance is a critical step in the data science process. Various evaluation metrics can be used, depending on the type of problem you are addressing. This phase helps in understanding how well the model works with unseen data and is important for ensuring the reliability and effectiveness of the model.

Based on the evaluation results, it might be necessary to fine-tune the model's parameters. This process, known as hyperparameter tuning, is essential to ensure that the model generalizes well to new, unseen data. The skill in hyperparameter tuning is honed through experience, practice, and experimenting with various parameter values.

Model Deployment

The deployment of a machine learning model is a pivotal phase in the data science lifecycle. Once stakeholders approve the model based on its performance, the focus shifts to making the model operational in a real-world environment. This process involves transitioning the model from a development setting on a local machine to a production environment where it can actively contribute to organizational decision-making. Luigi Patruno aptly states, "no machine learning model is useful unless it's deployed to production." The deployment process enables the model to deliver practical, data-driven insights and becomes accessible to end-users.

This phase often involves intricate coordination between data scientists, business professionals, software engineers, and IT teams, aiming to integrate the model seamlessly with existing business processes and systems.

Model Maintenance and Optimization

After deploying a model, ongoing maintenance and optimization become important . The notion that a data scientist's job ends with deployment is a misconception. In reality, like any sophisticated system, machine learning models require regular maintenance and updates to stay effective.

One key reason for this necessity is the dynamic nature of data and environments in which models operate. For example, the Covid-19 pandemic significantly changed customer behaviors and patterns, demonstrating the need for models to be updated to reflect these new realities. Models that aren't periodically updated may lose their predictive accuracy and relevance.

Organizations need to adopt a strategy for continuous model maintenance and optimization. This strategy typically involves regular updates of the data sets and retraining of the models to adapt to new trends and patterns. These updates might be scheduled at regular intervals depending on the specific needs and dynamics of the business and its environment.

www.ingramcontent.com/pod-product-compliance
Lightning Source LLC
La Vergne TN
LVHW051713050326
832903LV00032B/4172